Top Skills

Vocabulary

For Selective Schools and
Scholarship Preparation

Therese Burgess

A
FIVE SENSES
PUBLICATION

To Myra Elizabeth, a most special girl.

Five Senses Education Pty Ltd
2/195 Prospect Highway
Seven Hills 2147
New South Wales
Australia

Burgess, Therese
Top Skills - Vocabulary
ISBN 978-1-74130-263-9

How to use this book.

Top Skills : Vocabulary is intended primarily as an aid for the Selective Schools and Scholarship exams. However, this book can be used productively by any upper primary student wishing to improve his or her vocabulary. It will provide a solid grounding in word skills which will be vital in secondary school.

The book consists of twenty units. Each unit begins with a vocabulary list and a cloze exercise. The topics covered in the remainder of the unit comprise all aspects of vocabulary. They include:

- Synonyms and antonyms
- Idioms
- Homophones
- Similes
- Frequently misused words
- Analogies
- Proofreading

The student should use this book in conjunction with their dictionary and thesaurus. Simply guessing at the meaning of words has no practical value.

Maximum value will be gained from this book by writing out corrections in the space provided at the back of the book. The parent should test the student on these corrections from time to time.

Consistent vocabulary practice will improve performance on vocabulary tests, help understanding in comprehension exercises and enhance writing skills.

UNIT ONE

*1. Choose the correct **meaning** for each word.*

a. saga

[ ] a long coat
[ ] a long story
[ ] a type of bird

b. keen

[ ] blunt
[ ] unreal
[ ] sharp

c. deteriorate

[ ] to grow worse
[ ] to make ill
[ ] to abuse

d. interred

[ ] discovered
[ ] suggested
[ ] buried

e. embellished

[ ] decorated
[ ] made bitter
[ ] covered

f. frenzy

[ ] grave sickness
[ ] hysterical rage
[ ] hopeless despair

g. replica

[ ] imitation
[ ] original
[ ] engraving

h. inlaid

[ ] carved
[ ] set into
[ ] removed

2. Use each of these words in the **cloze**.

frenzy	designs	replicas	unearthed	copper
interred	sagas	keen	helmets	deteriorated

Viking warriors prized their weapons. Swords were sharpened to provide a _____ edge, and the hilts were often embellished with _____ or inlaid with other metals, such as _____ When he died, a warrior's armour and weapons were _____ with him, and many have been _____ by archaeologists. _____, often being made of leather, are usually found to have _____ and so only _____ are shown in museums. In Viking _____ we can read about warriors who worked themselves into a _____ before going into battle.

3. Match each **idiom** with its correct meaning.

- To be on the warpath.
- To cross swords.
- To have a fighting chance.
- To be in the wars.

a. To have a chance of success: _____

b. To disagree or quarrel: _____

c. To be very angry: _____

d. To be (slightly) injured. _____

4. Use a **form** of the word in brackets in each sentence. Your dictionary will help.

a. The Viking craftsman _____ the hilt of the sword with complicated patterns. (embellish)

b. The Viking warrior plunged into battle with _____ cries. (frenzy)

c. The archaeologist was dismayed at the _____ of the helmet. (deteriorate)

d. When he was _____, the warrior's weapons were buried with him. (inter)

e. Many great Norse _____ were written about brave deeds. (saga)

5. Choose the word which best resembles the **sound** the object makes. (**Onomatopoeia**)

tramp	ping	twang	roar	beat

a. The _____ of feet.

b. The _____ of battle.

c. The _____ of a drum.

d. The _____ of a bullet.

e. The _____ of a bow.

6. Match each word with a suitable **synonym**.

| saga | deteriorate | embellish | unearth | replica | frenzy |

a. adorn _____

b. excavate _____

c. degenerate _____

d. facsimile _____

e. legend _____

f. madness _____

7. Select the best **antonym**.

a. deteriorate   [ ] stabilise [ ] improve [ ] decay

b. frenzy   [ ] rage   [ ] calm   [ ] confidence

8. Match each **collective noun** with its group.

| battalion | quiver | paddling | field | nest |

a. A _____ of ducks.

b. A _____ of runners.

c. A _____ of machine guns.

d. A _____ of arrows.

e. A _____ of soldiers.

UNIT TWO

*1. Choose the correct **meaning** for each word.*

a. picturesque

[ ] drawn roughly by hand
[ ] pleasant and interesting to look at
[ ] part of a picture

b. endure

[ ] die slowly
[ ] exhale
[ ] last, survive

c. fortified

[ ] strengthened
[ ] lengthened
[ ] conquered

d. ornate

[ ] massive
[ ] elaborate
[ ] historical

e. linear

[ ] built in stone
[ ] with many storeys
[ ] arranged in lines

f. imposing

[ ] grand, impressive
[ ] towering
[ ] compact, small

g. strategic

[ ] military
[ ] having some advantage
[ ] untried

h. concentric

[ ] one circle overlapping another
[ ] two circles side by side
[ ] one circle inside another

2. Use each of the words in the **cloze**.

drawbridge	endure	fortified	ornate	moat
linear	grand	strategic	concentric	ruins

Some _____ castles have been kept in good condition and modern day visitors can enjoy their _____ rooms, but others are now little more than picturesque _____. The early castles were just _____ homes which enjoyed a _____ position on a hill. The design of some castles is a _____ one, with all the rooms one after another in a line. Others have been constructed in _____ circles. Coupled with a surrounding _____ and accessed by a _____, these castles were easily defended and were able to _____ a long siege.

3. Complete the **analogies**.

a. **Knight** is to **castle** as **teacher** is to _____.

b. **Quiver** is to **arrow** as **flock** is to _____.

c. **Boot** is to **foot** as _____ is to **head**.

d. **Tower** is to **castle** as **steeple** is to _____.

e. **Cannonball** is to **cannon** as _____ is to **bow**.

f. **High** is to **low** as **ancient** is to _____.

g. **Cup** is to **tea** as _____ is to **soup**.

4. Look up the **meanings** of these words which are all related to those in the word list.

- stratagem: _____

- lineage: _____

- imposition: _____

- endurance: _____

- ornament: _____

- fort: _____

5. Use each of the **words above** in the correct sentence.

a. The defenders of the castle showed great _____ in withstanding the long siege.

b. Eventually, the attackers used a clever _____ to gain entry to the castle.

c. The _____ of heavy fines on the offenders reduced graffiti on the ancient walls.

d. Many tourists visit this ancient _____ every year.

e. The _____ of the nobles who lived in this castle went back a thousand years.

f. The duke employed many fine craftsmen to _____ the walls and ceilings of his castle.

6. *Choose the most suitable* **antonym** *for each word.*

a. endure   [ ] survive   [ ] collapse   [ ] frighten

b. ornate   [ ] official   [ ] fussy   [ ] plain

c. picturesque   [ ] dull   [ ] scenic   [ ] beautiful

d. imposing   [ ] huge   [ ] ordinary   [ ] majestic

7. *Match each person or creature with its* **home.**

noble	nun	soldier
Inuit	squirrel	tiger

a. convent: _____   d. lair: _____

b. igloo: _____   e. drey: _____

c. castle: _____   f. barracks: _____

8. *Use either* **there, their** *or* **they're** *in these sentences.*

a. The defenders of the castle had to quickly pull up _____ drawbridge before the riders arrived.

b. Close to the city, _____ are the ruins of two castles.

c. "It appears that _____ getting ready to attack!" warned the commander

UNIT THREE

1. Choose the correct **meaning** for each word.

a. focus

[ ] interior
[ ] area surrounding
[ ] centre of interest

b. havoc

[ ] severe flood
[ ] devastation, chaos
[ ] complete change

c. fissure

[ ] sharp vibration
[ ] crack, split
[ ] unbearable noise

d. ebbing

[ ] becoming more
[ ] staying the same
[ ] becoming less

e. lubricate

[ ] oil or grease
[ ] release quickly
[ ] flow freely

f. tremor

[ ] sliding sideways
[ ] trouble
[ ] vibration, trembling

g. accumulate

[ ] die away
[ ] increase steadily
[ ] deserve blame

h. magnitude

[ ] chaos, confusion
[ ] uproar
[ ] strength, greatness

2. Use each of the words in the **cloze**.

fissures	havoc	ebbing	magnitude	epicentre
underground	lubricate	tremors	accumulated	fault

If there is nothing to _____ the rocks along a
_____ line, they may stick together and pressure will
build up. Eventually, the _____ pressure is released in
a sudden, violent jerk known as an earthquake. The point of origin
of an earthquake is known as the focus and it may be deep
_____. The spot on the surface directly above is called
the _____. Earthquakes cause _____ which
may be sharp vibrations causing _____ or they may be
rolling waves like the _____ sea. Sometimes, the earth
splits open in _____, destroying roads and train
tracks. The _____ of an earthquake is measured by
the Richter Scale.

3. Match each **idiom** with its meaning.

- As steady as a rock.
- No great shakes.
- A mover and shaker.
- At a low ebb.

a. Someone who gets things done:_____

b. Unmoving, dependable: _____

c. Not very good or important: _____

d. Not feeling well: _____

4. *Use a **form** of the word in brackets in each sentence. Your **dictionary** will help.*

a. Lack of _____ causes rocks to stick together. (lubricate)

b. The huge waves caused by the tsunami seemed at last to be _____ away. (ebb)

c. A number of _____ followed each other. (tremor)

d. It seemed that the earthquake was _____ in a very populated area. (focus)

e. After the earthquake the scene was one of total _____ (devastate)

f. The _____ conditions were not helped by the heavy rain. (chaos)

*5. Match each **occupation** with its field of work.*

| seismologist | joiner | botanist | optician | steeplejack |

a. A worker with wood: _____

b. A person who investigates earthquakes: _____

c. A person who studies plants: _____

d. A person qualified to prescribe glasses: _____

e. A person who fixes chimneys: _____

6. Match each word with a suitable **synonym**.

focus	tremor	magnitude	havoc
fissure	fault	lubricate	ebb

a. fade _____

b. crevice _____

c. confusion _____

d. greatness _____

e. grease _____

f. shaking _____

g. target _____

h. weakness _____

7. Write the **plurals** for each of these words.

a. focus: _____

b. lurch: _____

c. volcano: _____

d. tsunami: _____

8. Earthquakes are sometimes referred to as 'quakes'. What are the **abbreviated** forms of these words?

a. gymnasium: _____

b. pianoforte: _____

c. violoncello: _____

d. telephone: _____

e. omnibus: _____

f. automobile: _____

g. Limited: _____

h. Mister: _____

UNIT FOUR

*1. Choose the correct **meaning** for each word.*

a. ancestor

[ ] one who lives at the same time
[ ] one who lives a long time
[ ] one from whom you are descended

b. domesticated

[ ] living in a house
[ ] tamed
[ ] living in the country

c. characteristic

[ ] distinguishing quality
[ ] personality
[ ] letter used in printing

d. antiquity

[ ] modern days
[ ] ancient times
[ ] second-hand goods

e. resemble

[ ] rebuke
[ ] look like
[ ] need urgently

f. species

[ ] variety
[ ] mammals
[ ] signs

g. diminutive

[ ] large
[ ] grand
[ ] tiny

h. wide-spread

[ ] scarce
[ ] common
[ ] active

2. Use each of the words in the *cloze*.

wide-spread	species	smaller	ancestors	reared
antiquity	characteristics	resemble	domesticated	jackass

A male donkey is called a _____, while a jennet is the name for a female one. Donkeys have been used as beasts of burden since _____, when our _____ tamed wild ones and put them to work. The main _____ of donkeys are long ears, a grey coat with a dark line along its back and its diminutive feet, _____ than a horse's. Today, in Africa, you can see _____ of wild asses which _____ zebras, but do not have any stripes. They are just like the ones which were _____ and tamed for work, by our forefathers so many thousands of years ago. If you visit southern Europe, you will see many _____ donkeys and they are also _____ in Asia and in Africa.

3. Complete the table of *masculine* and *feminine* words.

Masculine	Feminine	Masculine	Feminine
jackass		bull	
gander		colt	
	hen		duck
	ewe		doe
stallion		billy-goat	

4. Look up the **meanings** of these words which are all related to the words in the word bank.

- antique: _____

- diminish: _____

- domestic: _____

- ancestry: _____

- specific: _____

- character: _____

5. Use each of the **words above** in the correct sentence.

a. The motorist tried to _____ his responsibility for the accident by blaming the other driver.

b. Tom says he can trace his _____ back to the First Fleet.

c. Grandpa always told me that working for what I wanted would build my _____.

d. I don't enjoy visiting _____ shops with my mother.

e. Please be more _____ about what you want me to do.

f. People who own large houses sometimes need to employ some _____ help.

6. *Choose the most suitable* **synonym** *for each word.*

a. ancestor   [ ] descendant   [ ] forefather   [ ] peer

b. domestic   [ ] lowly   [ ] employed   [ ] household

c. diminutive   [ ] tiny   [ ] lesser   [ ] shrunken

7. *Match each animal with its* **quality** *to complete each* **simile**.

mule	lamb	mouse	beaver
eel	tortoise	owl	lion

a. as slow as a   _____   e. as quiet as a   _____

b. as obstinate as a _____   f. as wise as an   _____

c. as slippery as an _____   g. as fierce as a   _____

d. as gentle as a   _____   h. as industrious as a _____

8. *Use either* **past** *or* **passed** *in these sentences.*

a. We _____ a man who was leading a donkey, laden with rolls of cloth.

b. In the _____, the donkey was a common means of transport.

c. The study of antiquities refers to _____ times.

UNIT FIVE

1. *Choose the correct* **meaning** *for each word.*

a. revival
  [ ] interest
  [ ] structure
  [ ] rebirth

b. patron
  [ ] person who sells art
  [ ] person who runs an art school
  [ ] person who helps an artist with expenses

c. revolution
  [ ] change
  [ ] explosion
  [ ] disorder

d. customary
  [ ] unusual
  [ ] usual
  [ ] useless

e. influential
  [ ] intelligent and studious
  [ ] having effect on others
  [ ] always certain

f. inspired
  [ ] excited or filled with enthusiasm
  [ ] interrupted
  [ ] overloaded with information

g. scholar
  [ ] teacher
  [ ] learner
  [ ] school

h. innovation
  [ ] close examination
  [ ] stress and strain
  [ ] new idea or method

2. Use each of the words in the **cloze**.

revival	painters	revolution	customary	life-like
influential	texts	inspired	innovation	printing

The Renaissance was a time when there was a _____ in the way people thought. The name 'Renaissance' means rebirth or _____.   People became very interested in art and wealthy patrons helped struggling _____. Artists began to paint pictures which were more _____. Sculptors, such as Michelangelo were _____ by the art of Ancient Greece and Rome, and produced many beautiful statues. Scholars also studied _____ from Greece and Rome. The invention of the _____ press helped to spread their ideas. Many _____ thinkers such as Machiavelli lived during this period.   It was a time when _____ ways of doing things were challenged, and was a time of great _____.

3. Match each **idiom** with its meaning.

- It's all Greek to me.
- To think up.
- Food for thought.
- Ahead of one's time.

a. Having advanced ideas: _____

b. I can't understand it: _____

c. Something to think about: _____

d. To invent something: _____

4. Use the **verb form** of the word in brackets to complete the sentence. Be careful with tense!

a. After a hot shower, the hikers felt quite _____.
   (revival)

b. The invention of the printing press _____ the
   reading of books. (revolution)

c. Looking at a beautiful painting might _____
   you to try painting. (inspiration)

d. If you want diners to _____ your restaurant, you
   must offer good service and great food. (patron)

e. The people with whom we mix _____ the way
   we think. (influential)

5. Match each **worker** with their tool or implement.

palette	theodolite	squeegee	saw
gavel	chisel	spanner	test tube

a. carpenter: _____   e. mechanic: _____

b. artist: _____   f. sculptor: _____

c. surveyor: _____   g. scientist: _____

d. window-cleaner: _____   h. judge: _____

6. Choose the best **synonym** for each word.

a. inspire: [ ] establish   [ ] excite   [ ] introduce

b. lifelike: [ ] dull   [ ] restless   [ ] realistic

c. influence: [ ] swelling   [ ] change   [ ] power

d. invent: [ ] create   [ ] construct   [ ] immerse

e. custom: [ ] period   [ ] tradition   [ ] work

f. revolutionary: [ ] different   [ ] correct   [ ] modern

g. patronising: [ ] friendly   [ ] pale   [ ] snobbish

h. revive: [ ] resist   [ ] refresh   [ ] repay

7. Select the correct **word** in each set of brackets.

a. The kiosk sold magazines as well as (stationary / stationery).

b. The resolution was passed by the (council / counsel) at the latest meeting.

c. In (vein / vain) we tried to change his mind.

d. At last the fog lifted and we were able to (proceed / precede).

e. After the armistice was signed, the countries enjoyed fifty years of (piece / peace).

f. Please don't read (allowed / aloud) as it is very distracting when I am trying to work

UNIT SIX

*1. Choose the correct **meaning** for each word.*

a. molten
[ ] solid
[ ] hardened
[ ] melted

b. erode
[ ] crack suddenly
[ ] wear away
[ ] destroy all traces of

c. gouge
[ ] scoop out
[ ] hold fast
[ ] strike hard

d. merge
[ ] fuse
[ ] pity
[ ] tingle

e. geologist
[ ] one who studies plants
[ ] one who studies earthquakes
[ ] one who studies rocks

f. esplanade
[ ] wide open road
[ ] type of French sword
[ ] meat dish

g. backdrop
[ ] trapdoor
[ ] background
[ ] dropout

h. battlement
[ ] army division
[ ] large dungeon below castle
[ ] castle wall with gaps along top

2. Use each of the words in the *cloze*.

battlements	esplanade	merged	eroded	million
molten	geologists	areas	backdrop	volcanic

Edinburgh Castle is built on _____ rock. We have been told by _____ how this strangely shaped rock came to be formed. About 340 _____ years ago, a huge volcanic explosion caused _____ rock to spread over the landscape. Later, during the Ice Age, huge sheets of ice _____ the soft rocks surrounding the volcano, but left the harder basalt in the centre. The ice flowed around this obstacle and gouged out the _____ which are now the main streets of the city of Edinburgh. Eventually the streams of ice _____ about a mile away from the 'castle rock'. The famous Edinburgh Military Tattoo is held on the _____ in front of the castle with the ancient building as a _____. The display always finishes with a lone piper playing on the _____.

3. Match the objects with their *country* of origin.

kilt	clogs	Uncle Sam
rose	beret	pasta

a. France: _____   d. Italy: _____

b. England: _____   e. America: _____

c. Holland: _____   f. Scotland: _____

4. **Proofread** this passage. There is a mistake in every line.
   Write the **corrections** in the box opposite.

In the dungeons of Edinburgh Castle, their is a
gun witch is known as Mons Meg. This huge
canon was built at Mons in Belgium in 1449. It
was a muzzle-loaded peace and soon saw battle.
Mons Meg was capable of fireing cannonballs of
150 kg. The problem with the gun was it's great
wait. It could only be dragged about 5 km a day.
On the last ocasion Mons Meg was fired, the gun
barel burst and it was simply abandoned.

5. *Choose the best* **synonym** *for each word.*

a. erode   [ ] obscure   [ ] destroy   [ ] vanish

b. merge   [ ] deserve   [ ] fuse   [ ] aid

c. military   [ ] army   [ ] navy   [ ] air force

d. display   [ ] hesitation [ ] exhibition   [ ] broadcast

6. *Words beginning with 'mill' have something to do with*
   thousands. Find the meaning of these 'mill' words.

a. millennium: _____

b. millipede: _____

c. millionaire: _____

7. Complete the table of **singular** and **plural**.

SINGULAR	PLURAL
volcano	
banjo	
	armies
	fish
hoof	
cupful	
	stimuli
	knives

8. Use either **to** or **too** in these sentences.

a. My grandfather intends _____ travel _____ Scotland in the new year.

b. When he lived in Edinburgh, he found the winters were _____ cold.

c. I wish that I could go, _____, as I have never travelled _____ anywhere exciting.

d. The weary tourists had been _____ many castles on their trip.

e. Do you like the porridge, or do you think that it's _____ salty?

f. _____ get _____ Holyrood Palace, walk from the Castle

_____ the end of the Royal Mile

UNIT SEVEN

*1. Choose the correct **meaning** for each word.*

a. legendary

[ ] brave
[ ] fictional
[ ] actual

b. vagabond

[ ] robber
[ ] wanderer
[ ] chief

c. tyrant

[ ] gifted leader
[ ] clever politician
[ ] cruel ruler

d. venison

[ ] meat from a pig
[ ] meat from a deer
[ ] meat from a bear

e. charismatic

[ ] charming
[ ] tricky
[ ] truthful

f. burly

[ ] plump
[ ] muscular
[ ] tall

g. ballad

[ ] large bird
[ ] crossbow
[ ] song

h. regent

[ ] ruler of a kingdom for another
[ ] ruler by force
[ ] unlawful ruler

2. Use each of these words in the *cloze*.

regent	burly	venison	vagabond	Sheriff
legendary	tyrant	ballads	outlaw	friar

Robin Hood was a _____ hero who lived the life of a _____ in Sherwood Forest in England. At this time, the king, Richard the Lion Heart was fighting in the Crusades and his brother John, a cruel _____ , was acting as the _____. Robin was a charismatic figure who defied John and his deputy, the _____ of Nottingham. The _____band he led included a _____, Tuck, and a _____ man who was called Little John. Sometimes, when things were going well for them, the outlaws enjoyed a feast of _____ and ale, and sang _____ about their exploits.

3. Match each *idiom* to the best sentence.

- To be on a crusade.
- A price on his head.
- To sing his praises.

a. The poor people whom Robin helped were very ready
   _____.

b. Robin knew that he had _____.

c. The Sheriff seemed _____ to capture Robin.

4. Use a **form** of the word in brackets in each sentence. The dictionary will help.

a. Many _____ have grown up about people performing heroic deeds. (legendary)

b. The _____ behaviour of the king eventually led to his downfall. (tyrant)

c. Many people were drawn to Robin by his _____. (charismatic)

d. Little John was much _____ than Robin was. (burly)

5. Pair words from the box to form **compound** words.

long	house	stone	high
way	set	light	sun
bow	shore	tomb	sea

a. _____   d. _____

b. _____   e. _____

c. _____   f. _____

6. What would you put in these **containers**?

a. A barrel?   _____   b. A sack?   _____

c. A punnet?   _____   d. A vat?   _____

7. *Choose the best **synonym** for each word.*

a. vagabond   [ ] outlaw   [ ] rover   [ ] leader

b. tyrant   [ ] bully   [ ] boss   [ ] monarch

c. burly   [ ] angry   [ ] lean   [ ] thick-set

d. legendary   [ ] mythical [ ] old   [ ] factual

e. charismatic   [ ] young   [ ] petty [ ] attractive

8. *Place each of these words in correct **alphabetical** order.*

sword shield longbow crossbow sheriff forest foe vagabond

_____

_____

9. *Circle the word which is **spelled** correctly.*

a.	fascenate	fascinate	fassinate	fascinait
b.	abbundant	abundent	abundant	abunndant
c.	accomplish	acomplish	ackomplish	acomplesh
d.	celerbrate	celebrait	celebrate	cellebrate
e.	consceince	conshience	conscence	conscience

UNIT EIGHT

1. *Choose the correct **meaning** for each word.*

a. quota
    [ ] result of division
    [ ] words repeated exactly
    [ ] number required

b. implements
    [ ] designs
    [ ] tools
    [ ] requirements

c. colossal
    [ ] immense
    [ ] difficult
    [ ] impossible

d. dilemma
    [ ] answer
    [ ] problem
    [ ] idea

e. arduous
    [ ] uncomplicated
    [ ] backbreaking
    [ ] effortless

f. knoll
    [ ] valley
    [ ] plain
    [ ] mound

g. uniform
    [ ] regular
    [ ] dull
    [ ] prescribed

h. toiled
    [ ] resisted strongly
    [ ] worked hard
    [ ] argued constantly

2. Use each of the words in the **cloze**.

uniform	quota	toiled	dilemmas	trenches
arduous	overlooking	implements	colossal	gangs

The building of the Great Pyramid at Gizeh was a _____ undertaking. With only the simplest of _____, the construction created many _____. The site chosen for the pyramid was a knoll _____ the surrounding plain. The builders used a system of water-filled _____ to make sure that the pyramid was constructed on a _____ base. Every village provided a _____ of workers who were then organised into _____ of about twenty. They _____ long hours and the work was _____. History has applauded their magnificent achievement.

3. Put these **nouns** into their correct category.

impala   leotard   chisel   awl   lynx   poncho

tapir   fedora   mallet   quokka   fez   spanner

Tools	Animals	Clothing

4. *Choose a better word for* **went** *in each of these sentences.*

| scurried | hobbled | strode | bounded | tottered |

a. The angry man _____ up to the complaints department.

b. When their grandparents arrived, the children _____ joyfully up to them.

c. The frail old lady _____ down her front path.

d. As they opened the door of the deserted house, a number of mice _____ across the floor.

e. With difficulty, the boy with the injured foot _____ into the casualty department.

5. *Add a* **prefix** *to each of these words to change their meaning.*

a. ____necessary

b. ____real

c. ____possible

d. ____loyal

e. ____noble

f. ____legal

g. ____patient

h. ____lawful

i. ____behave

6. *Complete the* **analogies**.

a. **Pharaoh** is to **Egypt** as _____ is to **America**.

b. **Steering wheel** is to **car** as **rudder** is to _____.

c. **Cheese** is to **cow** as **bacon** is to _____.

7. Complete the table.

Noun	Verb	Adjective	Adverb
construction		constructive	
	beautify		
puzzle			
	civilise		
attraction			
	---------------	intelligent	
			tirelessly
strength			

8. Choose the correct **word** in each set of brackets to complete the sentence.

a. The Pharaoh's coffin was taken on (bored / board) the royal barge.

b. The ancient Egyptians understood the (principal / principle) of the pulley.

c. At (knight / night) the workers were usually exhausted.

d. A (council / counsel) of elders supervised the construction.

e. The Pyramid has a profound (affect / effect) on all who see it.

9. In which **countries** would you find these leaders?

a. Sultan: _____

b. Chancellor: _____

c. Rajah: _____

UNIT NINE

*1. Choose the correct **meaning** for each word.*

a. notorious

[ ] necessary
[ ] having a bad reputation
[ ] significant

b. emissions

[ ] substances taken in
[ ] substances given out
[ ] substances used in industry

c. potential

[ ] possibility
[ ] consequence
[ ] cause

d. speculation

[ ] concern
[ ] theories
[ ] surprise

e. induced

[ ] transported
[ ] put away
[ ] caused

f. noxious

[ ] of no importance
[ ] poisonous or harmful
[ ] interfering

g. urbanisation

[ ] creation of farmland
[ ] preservation of old buildings
[ ] growth of cities

h. catastrophe

[ ] massive change
[ ] beneficial result
[ ] huge disaster

2. Use each of the words in the **cloze**.

catastrophe	global	induced	potential	notorious
speculation	noxious	emissions	atmosphere	loss

There is much _____ about the likely consequences of _____ warming on our planet. This increase in temperature has been _____ by a rise in the 'greenhouse' gases present in the _____. The most _____ of these gases is carbon dioxide. Its increase is linked to greater urbanisation and the _____ of many forests. The _____ from factories as well as the fumes produced by motor vehicles, add to the amount of _____ gases in the atmosphere. If we do not take steps now, global warming has the _____ to create a huge _____ for Earth.

3. Match each **idiom** to the best sentence.

- Raining cats and dogs.
- An Indian summer.
- As warm as toast.

a. We enjoyed _____ that year and were able to swim in May.

b. Mum tucked me up in a blanket with a cup of hot chocolate and I was _____.

c. It was _____ and the soccer match was cancelled.

4. *Use a **form** of the word in brackets in each sentence.*

a. As the motor whirred, it _____ a dense blue smoke. (emission)

b. Global warming could have _____ results for our planet. (catastrophe)

c. My cousins have moved from a rural area to an _____ one. (urbanisation)

d. We can only _____ about what the results of global warming may be. (speculation)

e. Sun-baking is a _____ dangerous activity as you may develop skin-cancer. (potential)

5. *Circle the word which is **opposite** to the word on the left.*

a. urban   -   suburb, rural, metropolitan, modern

b. noxious   -   toxic, unusual, injurious, beneficial

c. notorious   -   famous, infamous, ripe, scandalous

d. speculation -   guesswork, opinion, facts, dialogue

6. *Write the **plurals** for each of these words.*

a. gas _____   f. factory _____

b. theory _____   g. process _____

c. century _____   h. surplus _____

7. Match each country with its **abbreviation**.

N.Z.	G.B.	U.S.A.	U.K.	U.A.E.

a. Great Britain: _____

b. United States of America: _____

c. New Zealand: _____

d. United Arab Emirates: _____

e. United Kingdom: _____

8. Use either **fewer** or **less** in these sentences.

a. It is crucial that _____ cars use the roads every day.

b. There seem to be _____ really cold days in winter now.

c. _____ wheat is grown in this area than formerly.

d. When I was a child, there were _____ houses this far from the city centre.

e. _____ factories in this area will improve the quality of the air.

f. Don't make the mistake of using _____ sunscreen when it is cloudy.

g. _____ people use oil for heating these days.

UNIT TEN

*1. Choose the correct **meaning** for each word.*

a. ominous

[ ] fierce
[ ] warning of future event
[ ] eating all foods

b. turbulence

[ ] confusion, movement
[ ] anger
[ ] association

c. eludes

[ ] refers
[ ] escapes
[ ] deprives

d. meteorologist

[ ] one who studies meteors
[ ] one who studies bodily functions
[ ] one who studies the weather

e. bewildered

[ ] amused
[ ] scruffy
[ ] puzzled

f. bizarre

[ ] a market
[ ] extremely strange
[ ] brightly coloured

g. supernatural

[ ] outstanding
[ ] beyond nature
[ ] uncertain

h. freakish

[ ] weird
[ ] dangerous
[ ] infrequent

2. Use each of the words in the **cloze**.

logical	frogs	supernatural	ominous	unpleasant
turbulence	eludes	meteorologists	bewildered	bizarre

We often know that a thunderstorm is likely because of the _____ clouds which gather. Travelling in a plane can be extremely _____during a storm because of _____. Occasionally, some freakish events occur during storms. _____ fish, sea-shells and even tadpoles fall from the sky. Some _____ have attempted to find a _____ explanation for this phenomenon, but the reason _____ them. They are just as _____ as the rest of us. People have sometimes thought that these _____ and mysterious happenings might have some _____ cause.

3. Complete the table of **animals** and their **babies**.

Animal	Baby
frog	
fox	
	fawn
	gosling
leopard	
seal	
	leveret
	piglet
eagle	
	owlet

4. **Proofread** this passage. There is a mistake in every line. Write the **corrections** in the box opposite.

Jack and Laura were planing an excursion for
the weekend so they were hopeing for fine
whether. But, on Friday morning, they woke
to the sound of rain. It continued to pore all
day and they feared they're plans would have
to be canceled. The children went to bed in a
glum mood on Friday night. What a supprise
awaited them on Saturday. The rain had past!
In a joyfull mood, they prepared for the trip.

5. Which **word** is out of place in each group? Circle it.

   a. bizarre, outlandish, humdrum, weird

   b. bewilder, confirm, baffle, perplex

   c. logical, sound, sensible, absurd

   d. turbulence, restfulness, upheaval, commotion

   e. supernatural, miraculous, worldly, mystic

6. Words beginning with 'super' mean 'above' or 'over'.
Look up the meaning of these 'super' words.

a. supercilious:

b. superfluous:

c. superlative

7. Match the animal with the **adjective** which describes it.

cat	dog	fox	cow	horse
lion	pig	wolf	sheep	eagle

a. ovine: _____

b. feline: _____

c. porcine: _____

d. leonine: _____

e. bovine: _____

f. canine: _____

g. aquiline: _____

h. vulpine: _____

i. equine: _____

j. lupine: _____

8. Use the correct **word** in each set of brackets.

a. The (lightening / lightning) flashed across the darkened sky.

b. A (pain / pane) of glass was broken by a hailstone.

c. After the tornado, the (scene / seen) was one of chaos.

d. The (principle / principal) damage seemed to occur around the shopping centre.

e. There is always a (pause / paws) in the middle of a cyclone, when the eye passes over.

f. The (root / route) the storm had followed across the town was indicated by the unroofed houses.

UNIT ELEVEN

*1. Choose the correct **meaning** for each word.*

a. phenomenon
[ ] an unreal vision
[ ] a distinct stage
[ ] a remarkable person or thing

b. fungi
[ ] plants without leaves or roots
[ ] plants with brightly coloured leaves
[ ] edible plants

c. hover
[ ] a vacuum cleaner
[ ] float
[ ] move jerkily

d. wane
[ ] fade
[ ] find fault
[ ] battle

e. credulous
[ ] disbelieving
[ ] willing to believe
[ ] unbelievable

f. saturated
[ ] sodden
[ ] passable
[ ] parched

g. lantern
[ ] hammer
[ ] compass
[ ] lamp

h. hypothesis
[ ] theory
[ ] experiment
[ ] story

2. Use each of the words in the **cloze**.

scientist	fungi	lantern	homestead	saturated
hovers	wanes	credulous	owl	phenomenon

In a valley in the Go-Go-Billi Ranges in New South Wales, an interesting _____ occurs. Occasionally, an orange light appears and _____ for a while. After a few moments, it circles the tumbledown _____in the valley and then gradually _____.   Some _____ people believe that the light is a ghost, but a _____ has suggested an interesting hypothesis. He says that an _____ or some other bird nested in a log which contained _____ covered in phosphorus. The bird's feathers became _____ with the luminous material and so it began to glow in the dark. Local people believe that the light is just someone carrying a _____, or else gas from a swamp nearby.

3. Match each **idiom** with its meaning.

- To come to light.
- To go out like a light.
- To hide one's light under a bushel.

a. To try to hide one's talents or abilities.

b. To go to sleep very quickly.

c. To be revealed.

4. Complete the table of **singular** and **plural**.

SINGULAR	PLURAL
phenomenon	
hypothesis	
theory	
fungus	
ox	
stimulus	
crisis	
radius	

5. Choose the best **antonym** for the word in bold.

a. The light appears to **hover** over the valley.
   [ ] hang   [ ] drift   [ ] alight

b. After a time the light begins to **wane**.
   [ ] diminish   [ ] enhance   [ ]lessen

c. Jon is a rather **credulous** person who is easy to trick.
   [ ] cynical   [ ] naïve   [ ] foolish

d. My coat was **saturated** by the heavy rain.
   [ ] waterlogged   [ ] sopping   [ ] dehydrated

6. Use each of these **words** in the correct sentence.

credible   incredible

a. Tim's story is _____ and I think it's nonsense.

b. I accept Ken's version because it's _____.

7. Complete these **similes** with the words from the box.

light	quick	soft	dry	straight
sweet	tough	thin	steady	warm

a. As _____ as a rock.

b. As _____ as dust.

c. As _____ as a feather.

d. As _____ as butter.

e. As _____ as an arrow.

f. As _____ as lightning.

g. As _____ as leather.

h. As _____ as honey.

i. As _____ as a rake.

j. As _____ as toast.

8. Choose the correct **word** in brackets to complete each sentence.

a. In the first year, the restaurant showed a good (prophet / profit).

b. The (imminent / eminent) statesman was given a welcome by the city.

c. My father is the (personnel / personal) manager for that company.

d. An artist uses a (palette / palate) on which to mix his paints.

e. My grandparents (immigrated / emigrated) from Ireland.

f. I really (loath / loathe) getting up on cold mornings.

g. My mother (formerly / formally) worked as a graphic designer.

UNIT TWELVE

*1. Choose the correct **meaning** for each word.*

a. garrison
  [ ] group of townspeople
  [ ] group of tradesmen
  [ ] group of soldiers

b. siege
  [ ] outer wall of a castle
  [ ] surrounding and bombarding of a place
  [ ] total defeat

c. objective
  [ ] result
  [ ] aim
  [ ] cause

d. intercept
  [ ] stop someone's progress
  [ ] connect two things
  [ ] pause for a moment

e. vulnerable
  [ ] sick and tired
  [ ] ready for action
  [ ] exposed to attack

f. demoralise
  [ ] discourage
  [ ] lead into wrongdoing
  [ ] blame unfairly

g. strategic
  [ ] important, vital
  [ ] elevated
  [ ] sensible

h. ricochet
  [ ] rebound from solid surface
  [ ] encircle
  [ ] rattle around

2. Use each of the words in the **cloze**.

ricochet	strategic	garrison	inhabitants	siege
defeat	enemy	intercept	objective	cannonballs

The April and June, 1644, the city of York was in a state of
_____. This situation followed the departure of the
city _____, who normally defended the city. They had
left to attempt to _____ some enemy forces and
had suffered a _____. The city of York was of great
_____ value to the enemy and as it was left in a
vulnerable position, the _____ forces lost no time in laying
siege to it. Their _____ was to try to demoralise the
_____ of the city. One of the ways they did this was to
fire _____ at the Minster, the main church while
people were at prayer. The cannonballs would often smash windows
and _____ around the inside of the church. Legend
has it that no-one was harmed!

3. Match each **collective noun** with the group it describes.

bench	cairn	index	fusillade

a. An _____ of names.

b. A _____ of shots.

c. A _____ of stones.

d. A _____ of magistrates.

4. Add either *ie* or *ei* to these words.

a. p _ _ ce

b. w _ _ gh

c. cit _ _ s

d. perc _ _ ve

e. dec _ _ ve

f. salar _ _ s

g. rec _ _ ver

h. trans _ _ nt

i. w _ _ ld

j. gr _ _ ve

k. w _ _ rd

l. repr_ _ ve

5. For each word on the left, choose a **synonym** from the brackets.

a. defeat   {advance, conquer, reinforce}

b. intercept   {merge, assure, obstruct}

c. vulnerable   {petite, defenceless, inconstant}

d. objective   {cause, score, goal}

e. strategic   {crucial, military, trivial}

6. Add prefixes to change these words into **antonyms**.

a. ___ interpret

b. ___believe

c. ___able

d. ___relevant

e. ___competent

f. ___personal

g. ___regard

h. ___behave

i. ___credit

j. ___written

k. ___print

l. ___sensitive

m. ___existent

n. ___stop

o. ___arm

7. Circle the word which is correctly *spelled*.

a. archertecture   architecture   archatecture

b. catheadral   cathedrel   cathedral

c. photograph   photergraph   photagrafe

d. nocternal   nocturnal   nocturnel

e. profesional   profeshional   professional

f. occurred   ocurred   occurred

g. asocciate   assoceate   associate

h. documentery   documentary   documentry

8. Use either *amount* or *number* in each sentence.

a. The _____ of archers in the city garrison was increased.

b. As time went on the _____ of food in the city dwindled.

c. A _____ of cannonballs landed within the church.

d. A large _____ of smoke was caused by the explosion.

e. The enemy raised a _____ of ladders against the city walls.

UNIT THIRTEEN

*1. Choose the correct **meaning** for each word.*

a. dynasty

[ ] criminal network
[ ] sequence of rulers
[ ] name for ancient kings

b. prosperity

[ ] a time of success and wealth
[ ] a time of conflict
[ ] a time of peace

c. feeble

[ ] ill
[ ] weak
[ ] small

d. statesman

[ ] governor of a state
[ ] citizen of a state
[ ] respected political leader

e. scholarship

[ ] teaching
[ ] learning
[ ] schools

f. civil

[ ] relating to the city
[ ] relating to the army
[ ] relating to citizens of the state

g. fortified

[ ] strengthened
[ ] army stronghold
[ ] walled in completely

h. dictator

[ ] ruler with complete power
[ ] ruler who loses power
[ ] ruler who consults parliament

2. Use each of the words in the *cloze*.

dictator	fortified	salaries	position	emperor
colleges	statesman	feeble	prosperity	dynasty

The first Ming _____of China and the founder of the Ming _____ was a bandit-chief named Hung Wu. He was able to take power away from the last Yuan emperor who had become very _____. Hung Wu ruled China for thirty years and proved to be a great _____. Although he was a fearsome _____ and executed anyone who opposed him, he brought _____ to the land. He moved his capital away from Beijing to the _____ city of Nanjing. He encouraged scholarship among the young men of the country and set up many _____. If they did well in their exams, they were rewarded with a_____ in the civil service, where they were sure of good _____.

3. Use each *idiom* correctly in a sentence.

- An iron fist.
- In the money.
- To strike while the iron was hot.

a. Hung Wu was able _____ and

seize control of the country.

b. For thirty years, he ruled China with _____.

c. The young man's position in the civil service meant that he was

_____.

4. Use an **adverb** formed from the word in brackets to complete each sentence.

a. The sick man moved his hand _____ (feeble).

b. If you want to pass this exam, you _____ must work harder. (simple)

c. In her painting, the colour changed _____ from red to yellow. (subtle)

d. My aunt spoke _____ to the impolite salesperson. (angry)

e. In the darkness, the thief crept _____ away from the scene. (stealthy)

f. There's plenty and you don't need to eat so _____. (greedy)

5. A person from **China** is a **Chinese** person. Write the correct adjective to describe each of these people.

a. A person from Holland: _____

b. A person from Iraq: _____

c. A person from Switzerland: _____

d. A person from Brazil: _____

e. A person from Greece: _____

f. A person from Portugal: _____

6. Match each **currency** from the box with its country of origin.

| lira | rupee | franc | rouble | yen | mark | guilder | pound |

a. Japan: _____

b. Russia: _____

c. Italy: _____

d. Germany: _____

e. Holland: _____

f. England: _____

g. India: _____

h. France: _____

7. Use either **practice** or **practise** in these sentences.

a. If you expect to do well in your piano exam, you will need to _____ more.

b. The night for netball _____ has been changed from Monday to Thursday.

c. It was Dad's usual _____ to make freshly squeezed orange juice each morning.

d. If you _____ your goal shooting, you are sure to improve.

e. Tara didn't _____ her speech although her teacher asked her to do this.

f. Frequent _____ will help your skills in any sport.

g. My little sister often refuses to _____ her flute.

UNIT FOURTEEN

*1. Choose the correct **meaning** for each word.*

a. medieval

[ ] the Stone Age
[ ] the Industrial Age
[ ] the Middle Ages

b. fictional

[ ] realistic
[ ] made-up
[ ] factual

c. site

[ ] vision
[ ] state
[ ] location

d. chivalrous

[ ] polite and honourable
[ ] tall and handsome
[ ] clever and witty

e. quest

[ ] query
[ ] mission
[ ] answer

f. goblet

[ ] cup
[ ] plate
[ ] knife

g. treacherous

[ ] full of plans
[ ] sly and dangerous
[ ] fierce, savage

h. futile

[ ] lengthy
[ ] fruitful
[ ] hopeless

2. Use each of the words in the **cloze**.

futile	quest	treacherous	site	fictional
hero	chivalrous	Round	goblet	possible

Tales of the medieval _____, King Arthur, have been popular for hundreds of years. It has never been _____ to prove that Arthur actually lived and we have to conclude that he was a _____ person. Arthur was the founder of the _____ Table, a group of knights famous for their courageous and _____ behaviour. Many of the knights were engaged in a _____ for the Holy Grail which was a _____ said to have been used at the Last Supper. This mission proved to be _____ as the Grail was never found. Arthur was killed by his _____ son, Mordred, and buried near the abbey of Glastonbury, a holy _____.

3. Complete the **analogies**.

a. **Knight** is to **lady** as **buck** is to _____.

b. **Horse** is to **stable** as **pig** is to _____.

c. **Bravery** is to **cowardice** as _____ is to **evil**.

d. **Table** is to **wood** as **window** is to _____.

e. **Wolf** is to **howls** as _____ is to **hoots**.

f. **Pack** is to **cards** as _____ is to **pups**.

4. Use the **noun** form of the word in brackets to complete each sentence.

a. The stories of King Arthur are works of _____ (fictional).

b. All were disgusted by the _____ of Arthur's son, Mordred. (treacherous)

c. The knights were famous for their _____ (chivalrous).

d.   At last, the knights recognised the _____ of their quest. (futile)

5. Match each **name** with its definition.

unicorn	quartet	bicycle	decade
solo	monologue	triplet	unicycle

a. Four people playing music together: _____

b. A period of ten years: _____

c. One person speaking: _____

d. Two-wheeled cycle: _____

e. Mythical animal with one horn: _____

f. One of three people born at the same time:_____

g. One person singing or playing an instrument:_____

h. One-wheeled cycle: _____

6. *Select the most suitable **antonym** for each word on the left.*

a. futile   {careless, useless, productive}

b. fictional   {imaginary, authentic, nonexistent}

c. chivalrous   {gallant, bold, impolite}

d. treacherous   {upright, repellent, deceitful}

7. *Replace **nice** in each sentence with a better word.*

mouth-watering	fragrant	friendly	becoming	well-chosen

a.   My mother wore a (nice) _____ dress to my cousin's wedding.

b.   I prefer flowers that have a (nice) _____ smell to those which are showy.

c.   I thanked Gran for the (nice) _____ gift she gave me for my birthday.

d.   Dad's special lasagna has a (nice) _____ aroma.

e.   The new girl at school has a (nice) _____ face.

UNIT FIFTEEN

*1. Choose the correct **meaning** for each word.*

a. compress

[ ] make up
[ ] express resentment
[ ] squeeze together

b. emits

[ ] takes in
[ ] warms up
[ ] sends out

c. immense

[ ] muscular
[ ] enormous
[ ] medium

d. buckle

[ ] bend out of shape
[ ] explode
[ ] swell outwards

e. tumultuous

[ ] covered with clouds
[ ] full of uproar and noise
[ ] dim and unclear

f. satellite

[ ] heavenly body which orbits another
[ ] any object sent into space
[ ] planet with rings

g. turmoil

[ ] hard work
[ ] confusion
[ ] destruction

h. withstand

[ ] escape from
[ ] stand up to
[ ] disbelieve

2. Use each of the words in the *cloze*.

withstand	turmoil	satellites	diameter	buckle
immense	emits	compresses	helium	protected

Jupiter is an _____ planet, the largest in the Solar System. Most of Jupiter is gas, hydrogen and _____.
The great pressure on Jupiter _____ the hydrogen into a liquid. This planet _____ heat radiation because it is still shrinking.   Space probes, sent there to explore, must be _____ from the radiation. The surface of Jupiter is always in a state of _____. Any probe sent into this tumultuous atmosphere will not be able to _____ the pressure for very long and will eventually _____.
Jupiter has a _____ of 142 980 kilometres.
Astronomers have, over time, discovered the existence of sixteen _____.

3. Match each *idiom* with its meaning.

- To see stars.
- To bring pressure to bear.
- A heatwave.
- Starry-eyed.

a. A period of very hot weather: _____

b. To see flashes of light as a result of a blow: _____

c. Full of naïve hope: _____

d. To try to force someone into action: _____

4. Put all of these words into **alphabetical** order.

asteroid	astronomer	space	star	atmosphere
gas	constellation	galaxy	probe	planet

_____

_____

5. Find both a **synonym** and an **antonym** for these words.

commotion   bear   colossal   expand   stillness

condense   defenceless   guarded   miniature   collapse

Word	Synonym	Antonym
compress		
protected		
withstand		
immense		
turmoil		

6. Choose the word which is **spelled** correctly.

a. gigantick   giggantic   gigantic

b. oxigen   oxygen   oxygin

c. eclipse   ecllipse   eclipes

d. temperiture   tempereture   temperature

7. Write a word which **describes** each group.

a. koala, possum, wombat   **<u>mammals</u>**

b. shirt, jacket, dress   _____

c. cup, plate, bowl   _____

d. petunia, rose, geranium   _____

e. car, motorcycle, truck   _____

f. oats, rye, wheat   _____

g. cod, flounder, bream   _____

h. coffee, water, juice   _____

8. Choose the most **appropriate** word in each set of brackets.

a. The (ascent / assent) of the mountain was widely praised.

b. I'm (confidant / confident) that I have a good chance in the race.

c. Our debating team has a full (compliment / complement) of speakers now.

d. The bad news had a terrible (affect / effect) on him.

e. The figure on the wall was merely an (illusion / allusion).

f. The soldier showed great (bravery / bravado) in battle.

UNIT SIXTEEN

*1. Choose the correct **meaning** for each word.*

a. zenith

[ ] lowest point
[ ] highest point
[ ] greatest depth

b. lagoon

[ ] small river flowing into larger one
[ ] soil dumped at mouth of river
[ ] shallow lake connected to larger one

c. shingle

[ ] coarse gravel
[ ] another name for 'quicksand'
[ ] clay and stones mixed

d. azure

[ ] silver
[ ] green
[ ] blue

e. kelp

[ ] long, thick grass
[ ] seaweed
[ ] root vegetable

f. halibut

[ ] a type of fish
[ ] a type of flower
[ ] a type of bird

g. mussels

[ ] small cakes
[ ] tools used by mechanics
[ ] shellfish

h. plover

[ ] a wanderer
[ ] coastal bird
[ ] craftsman working with hides

2. Use each word in the *cloze*.

shingle	plover	azure	halibut	panorama
zenith	mussels	lagoon	inspection	kelp

As we came to the top of the hill, a wonderful _____ was spread out before us. In the _____ sky, the sun had climbed to its _____. We walked beside the reed-fringed _____ and smelt the salt tang of the nearby sea. Startled by our approach, a _____ flew up with a whirr of wings.   A few picnickers made their way carefully over the sharp _____ of the beach.   Piles of _____ lay here and there, evidence of a recent storm. On the old jetty, the fishermen had spread out their catch for the _____of buyers. It included a great number of fish, including _____ and several types of shellfish, such as cockles and _____.

3. Put each of these words into their correct *category*.

dahlia gnat elm haddock plaice iris midge

maple rowan louse skate peony poplar

cricket pike aster earwig sole sycamore lotus

Trees	Flowers	Insects	Fish

4. The 'whirr of wings' is an example of **onomatopoeia**. Underline the examples of **onomatopoeia** in these sentences. (There may be more than one in each sentence.)

a. We were excited by the skirl of the bagpipes and the beat of the drums at the military tattoo.

b. The caw of a crow is an unpleasant sound.

c. As we left, the automatic door shut with a soft hiss.

d. My apartment is downtown and the roar of the traffic and the rumble of the trains sometimes keeps me awake.

e. A breeze rustles the leaves and raindrops patter on the roof.

5. Add either **able** or **ible** to these words.

a. adapt_____   e. vis_____   i. compar_____

b. divis_____   f. gull_____   j. aud_____

c. break_____   g. valu_____   k. ed_____

d. cap_____   h. access_____   l. sale_____

6. What do these people do? Use your **dictionary**.

a. bursar: _____

b. busker: _____

c. compere: _____

7. *Choose the correct **word** in each set of brackets.*

a. The army was able to (rest / wrest) control of the town from the opposing forces.

b. The builder used a (plum / plumb) line to make sure the walls were vertical.

c. If you are (lax / lacks) in doing your homework, your schoolwork will suffer.

d. The (loot / lute) is a very old stringed instrument.

e. At Hampton Court Palace, there is a famous (maize / maze).

f. My brother failed to obtain his motorcycle (license / licence).

8. *Use a better word for **said** in each sentence.*

admitted	warned	yawned	scoffed	denied

a. "I'm just exhausted," _____ Mum, putting down her book.

b. "Do you really think you have any chance?" _____ the older boy.

c. "Yes, I did break your vase," _____ Terry, "I'm so sorry."

d. "No, I didn't take it," _____ the tearful girl.

e. "Be careful with that hot chocolate!" _____ Dad.

UNIT SEVENTEEN

*1. Choose the correct **meaning** for each word.*

a. sustain
      [ ] dry out
      [ ] prolong, maintain
      [ ] accompany

b. habitat
      [ ] customs
      [ ] natural home
      [ ] created environment

c. industrious
      [ ] related to manufacturing
      [ ] busy and tireless
      [ ] annoyingly fussy

d. prudent
      [ ] impulsive and restless
      [ ] thrifty and saving
      [ ] wise and careful

e. variegated
      [ ] of many kinds
      [ ] of many colours
      [ ] of many sizes

f. crustacean
      [ ] member of the spider family
      [ ] hard-shelled aquatic animal
      [ ] animal living in a colony

g. comprise
      [ ] form an agreement
      [ ] contain, include
      [ ] blend thoroughly

h. predecessor
      [ ] descendant
      [ ] creator
      [ ] ancestor

2. Use each of the words in the *cloze*.

sustains	habitat	industrious	crustaceans	predecessor
spectacular	prudent	variegated	comprises	treasure

The Great Barrier Reef rests on its ancient _____, another weathered and eroded reef. The _____ Reef has been formed by _____ little animals called coral polyps.   Their labours over millennia have produced the _____ corals which delight us so much.   The coral forests are a protective _____ which _____ thousands of species of fish, plants and _____.   The reef system _____ reefs, lagoons, islands, estuaries and beaches. If we wish to preserve this national _____ for future generations, it would be _____ for us to take steps now to prevent anything which could damage it.

3. Use each *idiom* in the correct sentence.

- All at sea.
- A busy bee.
- A big fish.

a. Our teacher is _____ in the international chess tournament scene.

b. I'm going to have to be _____ if I want to get the house cleaned up before Mum gets home.

c. When he started at a new school in the country, Ian was _____ for a while.

4. *Sort all the names for **colours** into their correct categories.*

jade	crimson	raven	sapphire	scarlet
azure	sable	olive	ruby	ebony
indigo	rose	ultramarine	pea	jet
cherry	grass	turquoise	coal	emerald

RED	BLUE	GREEN	BLACK

5. *Choose the best **synonym** from the words on the right.*

a. industrious: {lifelike, relaxed, active}

b. variegated: {bright, shining, dappled}

c. spectacular: {impressive, expansive, twinkling}

d. prudent: {impulsive, far-sighted, hopeful}

e. habitat: {routine, nourishment, abode}

f. sustain: {collapse, support, request}

6. Write the **plural** of each word. Use your **dictionary** if you are not sure.

a. estuary: _____   e. authority: _____

b. tributary: _____   f. beach: _____

c. plateau: _____   g. photo: _____

d. shelf: _____   h. crisis: _____

7. Write two **antonyms** for each of these words.

a. prudent: _____

b. sustain: _____

c. industrious: _____

8. Complete each of these common **sayings** with a word from the box.

dried	easy	baggage	take
grey	ruin	fro	sound

a. bag and _____   e. to and _____

b. old and _____   f. rack and _____

c. give and _____   g. safe and _____

d. cut and _____   h. free and _____

UNIT EIGHTEEN

*1. Choose the correct **meaning** for each word.*

a. derelict
    [ ] intoxicated
    [ ] small and cramped
    [ ] falling into ruins

b. solitary
    [ ] alone, single
    [ ] silver-white in colour
    [ ] tired and drowsy

c. admonish
    [ ] answer rudely
    [ ] free from blame
    [ ] rebuke strongly

d. furtively
    [ ] in a sly manner
    [ ] quickly
    [ ] irresponsibly

e. compelled
    [ ] interrupted
    [ ] prevented from doing
    [ ] forced to do

f. barricade
    [ ] large flag
    [ ] barrier or fence
    [ ] criminal lawyer

g. recuperate
    [ ] rest and relax
    [ ] recover from illness
    [ ] remain in bed

h. wraith
    [ ] anger
    [ ] ghost
    [ ] ring of flowers

2. Use each of the words in the **cloze**.

recuperate	compelled	barricade	furtively	solitary
derelict	admonish	wraith	apartments	rumours

In our town there is a _____ house close by where I
live. It is the _____ house left in the street as all the
rest have been demolished to make way for _____.
It is regarded as unsafe and a _____ has been
erected to discourage people from entering it.   There are many
_____ that the house is haunted and for a long time I
have felt _____ to investigate it for myself. One day,
I climbed carefully over the barrier and _____ crept
inside.   Something suddenly appeared in front of me!   Was it a
_____? In my haste to escape, I fell while scrambling
over the barricade and broke my leg.   I took a long time to
_____ and my mother never lost an opportunity to
soundly _____ me.

3. Match each **mythical creature** with its definition.

centaur	minotaur	gorgon	werewolf	cyclops

a. A creature whose glance turned one to stone:_____

b. Half man, half horse:_____

c. One-eyed giant:_____

d. Half man, half bull:_____

e. A person changed into a wolf:_____

4. Proofread this passage. There is a **mistake** in every line. Write the corrections in the box opposite.

There had always been wierd rumours about
the house. My desision to investigate it came
out of a desire to prove I was couragous. My
friends wisely refused to acommpany me but
I resolved to go nonetheless. They where just
cowards, I told myself as I approched the door.
The creak of it's opening sounded very loud in
the empty house. I wont be afraid, I told myself as I creeped down the dim, dusty hallway.
Suddenly, their was a resounding crash and I
took to my heals and rushed out of the house.

5. Complete the sentences with **words** from the box.

cotton	weapons	whisky	grain	documents	money

a. We saw _____ being made in the distillery.

b. In the ginnery, _____ was being processed.

c. _____ is stored in a strong-room.

d. Many _____ were piled up in the armoury.

e. After the harvest, the _____ is stored in a silo.

f. We looked in the archives for the _____.

6. Add either **er** or **or** to each word.

a. act_ _   d. doct_ _   g. sens_ _   j. sail_ _

b. design_ _   e. competit_ _   h. gaol_ _   k. eras_ _

c. build_ _   f. crusad_ _   i. finish_ _   l. constrict_ _

7. Circle the word which is correctly **spelled**.

a. apearance	appearance	appearance
b. hankerchief	hankerchefe	handkerchief
c. skilful	skillful	skilfull
d. embarassed	embarrased	embarrassed
e. propellor	propeller	propellar

8. Use either **between** or **among** in each sentence.

a. Try to divide the food evenly _____ the two boys.

b. _____ you and me, she is not to be trusted.

c. Share these sweets _____ the whole class.

d. _____ six people, this food will not go far.

e. It's very difficult to distinguish _____ Tim and Dan, as they are so alike.

UNIT NINETEEN

*1. Choose the correct **meaning** for each word.*

a. shrewd
    [ ] slow-moving
    [ ] uncanny, odd
    [ ] smart and cunning

b. cajole
    [ ] coax, persuade
    [ ] gently mock
    [ ] disbelieve completely

c. hooligan
    [ ] rowdy young person
    [ ] crabby old person
    [ ] noisy spirit

d. audacity
    [ ] foolishness
    [ ] boldness, daring
    [ ] agreeableness

e. insinuate
    [ ] suggest indirectly
    [ ] propose or plan
    [ ] check closely

f. articulate
    [ ] able to foresee consequences
    [ ] able to express oneself clearly
    [ ] able to forgive easily

g. elude
    [ ] argue brilliantly
    [ ] laugh loudly
    [ ] escape by cleverness

h. wary
    [ ] upset
    [ ] cautious
    [ ] impressed

3. Use each of the words in the **cloze**.

audacity	insinuate	hooligan	elude	cajole
shrewd	wary	articulate	wisdom	trouble

Tom and Brad were friends. Tom was a very _____ type of person and he often persuaded Brad to embark with him on schemes of great _____. Brad was often doubtful about the _____ of these schemes but Tom usually managed to _____ him into participating. If coaxing didn't work, he would _____ that Brad was a coward. On the rare occasions that they landed in _____, Brad could always count on Tom's _____ explanations of what they were doing, to enable them to _____ punishment. Brad's parents were _____ of their son's friend, whom they regarded as a _____ .

3. Choose a suitable **antonym** for each of these words.

a. elude   {dodge, seize, flee}

b. articulate   {hesitant, well-spoken, arrogant}

c. wisdom   {insight, foolishness, tolerance}

d. cowardice   {fearfulness, graciousness, daring}

e. rare   {unusual, prompt, popular}

f. condemn   {approve, denounce, blame}

g. wary   {watchful, thoughtless, precise}

4. Add either **ous** or **ious** to each of these words.

a. courage_____   f. ambigu_____

b. ambit_____   g. advantage_____

c. gener_____   h. anonym_____

d. fam_____   i. ser_____

e. consc_____   j. var_____

5. Match each **collective noun** with its group.

truss	squadron	throng	range
index	archipelago	cairn	canteen

a. A _____ of stones.

b. A _____ of people.

c. An _____ of islands.

d. A _____ of planes.

e. An _____ of names.

f. A _____ of mountains.

g. A _____ of straw.

h. A _____ of cutlery.

6. A **euphemism** is a gentler or more polite way of saying something. Match each **euphemism** with its meaning.

- passed away
- stout
- intoxicated
- elderly
- outspoken

a. My uncle is often **rude** in his comments. _____

b. Since Grandma has stopped walking so often, she has become quite **fat**. _____

c. When people become **old**, their memory often deteriorates. _____

d. Mr Brown **died** last week. _____

e. Uncle Joe was rather **drunk** at the wedding. _____

7. Choose the **correct** word in each set of brackets.

a. We really enjoyed the (review / revue) put on by the local drama club.

b. It was a mistake to make such an unreliable person into your (confident / confidant).

c. My uncle is an (interstate / intestate) truck driver.

d. This is the site of an (interment / internment) camp during the last war.

e. I have always regarded him as a very (morale / moral) person.

UNIT TWENTY

*1. Choose the **correct** meaning for each word.*

a. belligerent
    [ ] indebted or obliged to do something
    [ ] hostile and aggressive
    [ ] inclined to do good

b. discord
    [ ] agreement
    [ ] musical notes
    [ ] disagreement

c. demented
    [ ] damp and soggy
    [ ] unbalanced, crazed
    [ ] unmistakeable

d. audacity
    [ ] boldness
    [ ] happiness
    [ ] control

e. bleak
    [ ] empty and vacant
    [ ] grim and gloomy
    [ ] peculiar and unusual

f. grisly
    [ ] shocking and terrible
    [ ] weak and shaky
    [ ] suspicious

g. strapping
    [ ] constantly fighting
    [ ] strong and robust
    [ ] fine and slender

h. wrath
    [ ] a ghost
    [ ] fury
    [ ] a shawl

2. Use each word in the *cloze*.

belligerent	demented	audacity	bleak	tale
strapping	grisly	discord	wrath	profoundly

When Henry VIII was a young man, he was reputed to be a handsome and _____ youth, intelligent and polite to all. However, as he aged, he changed _____. He became a stout and _____ man, used to having his own way at all costs. Anyone who disagreed with him felt the full force of his _____and could expect to spend time in the _____ Tower, surrounded by four cold stone walls. Henry would not tolerate any _____ caused by his wives, either, and two of them met a _____ fate, having their heads removed by the executioner's axe. Only one of them, the last one, had the _____ to answer back and lived to tell the _____. Some people have concluded that Henry must have been _____.

3. Put each *idiom* into the appropriate sentence.

- Lose your head.
- Heads will roll.
- Head over heels.

a. I think that my brother is _____ in love.

b. You mustn't _____ in a difficult situation.

c. If this project isn't successful, _____!

4. Match each word with **two** suitable **synonyms**.

ghastly	desolate	muscular	insane	aggressive
hostile	sturdy	deranged	dreary	terrifying

a. strapping: _____

b. grisly: _____

c. belligerent: _____

d. bleak: _____

e. demented: _____

5. Complete the table of **masculine** and **feminine** forms.

MASCULINE	FEMININE
duke	
baron	
	countess
emperor	
	hostess
	witch
priest	
brother-in-law	
lad	
	madam
	goddess

6. *Supply the correct **person** to complete each **simile**.*

king	hatter	babe	queen	judge
Job	sentinel	miser	thieves	Methuselah

a. As thick as _____.

b. As happy as a _____.

c. As mad as a _____.

d. As sober as a _____.

e. As mean as a _____.

f. As stately as a _____.

g. As old as _____.

h. As helpless as a _____.

i. As patient as _____.

j. As watchful as a _____.

7. *Choose the **correct** word in each set of brackets.*

a. I don't know (whose / who's) jacket this is, do you?

b. The lioness did not move far from (it's / its) den.

c. (There's / Their's) no reason to change our plans.

d. The police car cruised slowly (passed /past) the house.

e. The shopping centre is (to / too) far to walk.

f. It seems that (fewer / less) students enrolled this year.

g. You must (practice / practise) if you want to improve.

h. I tried to divide the cakes evenly (between / among) the girls.

ANSWERS

Unit One:
1. a. a long story b. sharp c. to grow worse d. buried e. decorate f. hysterical rage g. imitation h. set into
2. keen, designs, copper, interred, unearthed, Helmets, deteriorated, replicas, sagas, frenzy
3. a. To have a fighting chance. b. To cross swords. c. To be on the warpath. d. To be in the wars.
4. a. embellished b. frenzied c. deterioration d. interred e. sagas
5. a. tramp b. roar c. beat d. ping e. twang
6. a. embellish b. unearth c. deteriorate d. replica e. saga f. frenzy
7. a. improve b. calm
8. a. paddling b. field c. nest d. quiver e. battalion

Unit Two:
1. a. pleasant and interesting to look at b. last, survive c. strengthened d. elaborate e. arranged in lines f. grand, impressive g. having some advantage h. one circle inside another
2. grand, ornate, ruins, fortified, strategic, linear, concentric, moat, drawbridge, endure
3. a. school / classroom b. sheep / birds c. cap / hat d. church e. arrow f. modern g. mug / bowl / plate
5. a. endurance b. stratagem c. imposition d. fort e. lineage f. ornament
6. a. collapse b. plain c. dull d. ordinary
7. a. nun b. Inuit c. noble d. tiger e. squirrel f. soldier
8. a. their b. there c. they're

Unit Three:
1. a. centre of interest b. devastation c. crack d. becoming less e. oil or grease f. vibration g. increase steadily h. strength
2. lubricate, fault, accumulated, underground, epicentre, tremors, havoc, ebbing, fissures, magnitude
3. a. A mover and a shaker. b. As steady as a rock c. No great shakes. d. At a low ebb.
4. a. lubrication b. ebbing c. tremors d. focused e. devastation f. chaotic
5. a. joiner b. seismologist c. botanist d. optician e. steeplejack
6. a. ebb b. fissure c. havoc d. magnitude e. lubricate f. tremor g. focus h. fault
7. a. foci / focuses b. lurches c. volcanos / volcanoes d. tsunami / tsunamis
8. a. gym b. piano c. cello d. phone e. bus f. auto g. Ltd h. Mr

Unit Four:

1. a. one from whom you are descended b. tamed c. distinguishing quality d. ancient times e. look like f. variety g. tiny h. common
2. jackass, antiquity, ancestors, characteristics, smaller, species, resemble, reared, domesticated, widespread
3. jackass, jennet (jenny); bull, cow; gander, goose; colt, filly; rooster, hen; drake, duck; ram, ewe; buck, doe; stallion, mare; billy-goat, nanny-goat
5. a. diminish b. ancestry c. character d. antique e. specific f. domestic
6. a. forefather b. household c. tiny
7. a. tortoise b. mule c. eel d. lamb e. mouse f. owl g. lion h. beaver
8. a. passed b. past c. past

Unit Five:

1. a. rebirth b. person who helps an artist c. change d. usual e. having effect on others f. excited g. learner h. new idea
2. revolution, revival, painters, life-like, inspired, texts, printing, influential, customary, innovation
3. a. Ahead of one's time. b. It's all Greek to me. c. Food for thought. d. To think up.
4. a. revived b. revolutionised c. inspire d. patronise e. influence
5. a. saw b. palette c. theodolite d. squeegee e. spanner f. chisel g. test tube h. gavel
6. a. excite b. realistic c. power d. create e. tradition f. different g. snobbish h. refresh
7. a. stationery b. council c. vain d. proceed e. peace f. aloud

Unit Six:

1. a. melted b. wear away c. scoop out d. fuse e. one who studies rocks f. wide, open road g. background h. castle wall with gaps at the top
2. volcanic, geologists, million, molten, eroded, areas, merged, esplanade, backdrop, battlements
3. a. beret b. rose c. clogs d. pasta e. Uncle Sam f. kilt
4. there, which, cannon, piece, firing, its, weight, occasion, barrel
5. a. destroy b. fuse c. army d. exhibition
7. volcanos / volcanoes; banjos / banjoes; army; fish; hooves / hoofs; cupfuls; stimulus; knife
8. a. to, to b. too c. too, to d. to e. too f. To, to, to

Unit Seven:

1. a. fictional b. wanderer c. cruel ruler d. meat from a deer e. charming f. muscular g. song h. ruler of a kingdom for another
2. legendary, vagabond, tyrant, regent, Sheriff, outlaw, friar, burly, venison, ballads
3. a. to sing his praises b. a price on his head c. to be on a crusade
4. a. legends b. tyrannical c. charisma d. burlier
5. Possible answers are: longbow, lighthouse, tombstone, seashore, highway, sunset
6. a. beer, water, oil b. flour, grain, potatoes c. strawberries d. wine, oil, cooking fat
7. a. rover b. bully c. thick-set d. mythical e. attractive
8. crossbow, foe, forest, longbow, sheriff, shield, sword, vagabond
9. a. fascinate b. abundant c. accomplish d. celebrate e. conscience

Unit Eight:

1. a. number required b. tools c. immense d. problem e. backbreaking f. mound g. regular h. worked hard
2. colossal, implements, dilemmas, overlooking, trenches, uniform, quota, gangs, toiled, arduous
3. TOOLS: chisel, awl, mallet, spanner
   ANIMALS: impala, lynx, tapir, quokka
   CLOTHING: leotard, poncho, fedora, fez
4. a. strode b. bounded c. tottered d. scurried e. hobbled
5. a. unnecessary b. unreal c. impossible d. disloyal e. ignoble f. illegal g. impatient h. unlawful i. misbehave
6. a. President b. boat / ship c. pig
7. construction, construct, constructive, constructively; beauty, beautify, beautiful, beautifully; puzzle, puzzle, puzzling, puzzlingly; civilisation, civilise, civil, civilly; attraction, attract, attractive, attractively; intelligence, intelligent, intelligently; tiredness, tire, tireless, tirelessly; strength, strengthen, strong, strongly
8. a. board b. principle c. night d. council e. effect
9. a. A Muslim country such as Brunei. b. A European country such as Germany. c. India

Unit Nine:

1. a. having a bad reputation b. substances given out c. possibility d. theories e. caused f. poisonous g. growth of cities h. huge disaster
2. speculation, global, induced, atmosphere, notorious, loss, emissions, noxious, potential, catastrophe
3. a. an Indian summer b. as warm as toast c. raining cats and dogs

4. a. emitted b. catastrophic c. urban d. speculate e. potentially
5. a. rural b. beneficial c. famous d. facts
6. a. gases b. theories c. centuries d. factories e. processes f. surpluses
7. a. G.B. b. U.S.A. c. N.Z. d. U.A.E. e. U.K.
8. a. fewer b. fewer c. less d. fewer e. Fewer f. less g. Fewer

Unit Ten:
1. a. warning of future event b. confusion c. escapes d. one who studies the weather e. puzzled f. extremely strange g. beyond nature h. weird
2. ominous, unpleasant, turbulence, Frogs, meteorologists, logical, eludes, bewildered, bizarre, supernatural
3. frog, tadpole; fox, cub; deer, fawn; goose, gosling; leopard, cub; seal, pup; hare, leveret; pig, piglet; eagle, eaglet; owl, owlet
4. planning, hoping, weather, pour, their, cancelled, surprise, passed, joyful
5. a. humdrum b. confirm c. absurd d. restfulness e. worldly
6. Consult dictionary.
7. a. sheep b. cat c. pig d. lion e. cow f. dog g. eagle h. fox i. horse j. wolf
8. a. lightning b. pane c. scene d. principal e. pause f. route

Unit Eleven:
1. a. remarkable person or thing b. plants without leaves or stems c. float d. fade e. willing to believe f. sodden g. lamp h. theory
2. phenomenon, hovers, homestead, wanes, credulous, scientist, owl, fungi, saturated, lantern
3. a. to hide one's light under a bushel b. to go out like a light c. to come to light
4. phenomena, hypotheses, theories, fungi, oxen, stimuli, crises, radii
5. a. alight b. enhance c. cynical d. dehydrated
6. a. incredible b. credible
7. a. steady d. dry c. light d. soft e. straight f. quick g. tough h. sweet i. thin j. warm
8. a. profit b. eminent c. personnel d. palette e. emigrated f. loathe g. formerly

Unit Twelve:
1. a. a group of soldiers b. surrounding and bombarding of a castle c. aim d. stop someone's progress e. exposed f. discourage g. important h. rebound
2. siege, garrison, intercept, defeat, strategic, enemy, objective, inhabitants, cannonballs, ricochet
3. a. index b. fusillade c. cairn d. bench

4. a. piece b. weigh c. cities d. perceive e. deceive f. salaries g. receiver h. transient i. wield j. grieve k. weird l. reprieve
5. a. conquer b. obstruct c. defenceless d. goal e. crucial
6. a. misinterpret b. disbelieve c. unable d. irrelevant e. incompetent f. impersonal g. disregard h. misbehave i. discredit j. unwritten k. misprint l. insensitive m. nonexistent n. non-stop o. disarm
7. a. architecture b. cathedral c. photograph d. nocturnal e. professional f. occurred g. associate h. documentary
8. a. number b. amount c. number d. amount e. number

Unit Thirteen

1. a. sequence of rulers b. time of success and wealth c. weak d. respected political leader e. learning f. relating to the city g. strengthened h. ruler with complete power
2. emperor, dynasty, feeble, statesman, dictator, prosperity, fortified, colleges, position, salaries
3. a. to strike while the iron was hot b. an iron fist c. in the money
4. a. feebly b. simply c. subtly d. angrily e. stealthily f. greedily
5. a. Dutch b. Iraqi c. Swiss d. Brazilian e. Greek f. Portuguese
6. a. yen b. rouble c. lira d. mark e. guilder f. pound g. rupee h.franc
7. a. practise b. practice c. practice d. practise e. practise f. practice g. practise

Unit Fourteen

1. a. the Middle Ages b. made-up c. location d. polite and honourable e. mission f. cup g. sly and dangerous h. hopeless
2. hero, possible, fictional, Round, chivalrous, quest, goblet, futile, treacherous, site
3. a. doe b. sty c. good d. glass e. owl f. litter
4. a. fiction b. treachery c. chivalry d. futility
5. a. quartet b. decade c. monologue d. bicycle e. unicorn f. triplet g. solo h. unicycle
6. a. productive b. authentic c. impolite d. upright
7. a. becoming b. fragrant c. well-chosen d. mouth-watering e. friendly

Unit Fifteen:

1. a. squeeze together b. sends out c. enormous d. bend out of shape e. full of uproar f. heavenly body which orbits another g. confusion h. stand up to
2. immense, helium, compresses, emits, protected, turmoil, withstand, buckle, diameter, satellites
3. a. a heatwave b. to see stars c. starry-eyed d. to bring pressure to bear

4. asteroid, astronomer, atmosphere, constellation, galaxy, gas, planet, probe, space, star
5. compress – condense, expand; protected – guarded, defenceless; withstand – bear, collapse; immense – colossal, miniature; turmoil – commotion, stillness
6. a. gigantic b. oxygen c. eclipse d. temperature
7. b. clothing c. crockery d. flowers e. motor vehicles / transport f. grains g. fish h. drinks / liquids
8. a. ascent b. confident c. complement d. effect e. illusion f. bravery

Unit Sixteen:
1. a. highest point b. shallow lake connected to a larger one c. coarse gravel d. blue e. seaweed f. a type of fish g. shellfish h. coastal bird
2. panorama, azure, zenith, lagoon, plover, shingle, kelp, inspection, halibut, mussels
3. TREES: elm, maple, rowan, poplar, sycamore
   FLOWERS: dahlia, iris, peony, aster, lotus
   INSECTS: gnat, midge, louse, cricket, earwig
   FISH: haddock, plaice, skate, pike, sole
4. a. skirl, beat b. caw c. hiss d. roar, rumble e. rustles, patter
5. a. adaptable b. divisible c. breakable d. capable e. visible f. gullible g. valuable h. accessible i. comparable j. audible k. edible l. saleable
6. Dictionary work.
7. a. wrest b. plumb c. lax d. lute e. maze f. licence
8. a. yawned b. scoffed c. admitted d. denied e. warned

Unit Seventeen:
1. a. prolong b. natural home c. busy d. wise e. of many colours f. hard-shelled aquatic animal g. contain h. ancestor
2. predecessor, spectacular, industrious, variegated, habitat, sustain, crustaceans, comprises, treasure, prudent
3. a. a big fish b. a busy bee c. all at sea
4. RED: crimson, scarlet, ruby, rose, cherry
   BLUE: sapphire, azure, indigo, ultramarine, turquoise
   GREEN: jade, olive, pea, grass, emerald
   BLACK: raven, sable, ebony, jet, coal
5. a. active b. dappled c. impressive d. far-sighted e. abode f. support
6. a. estuaries b. tributaries c. plateaux d. shelves e. authorities f. beaches g. photos h. crises
7. Possible antonyms: a. foolish, unwise b. undermine, destroy c. lazy, idle
8. a. baggage b. grey c. take d. dried e. fro f. ruin g. sound h. easy

Unit Eighteen:
1. a. falling into ruins b. alone c. rebuke strongly d. in a sly manner e. forced to do f. barrier g. recover from illness h. ghost
2. derelict, solitary, apartments, barricade, rumours, compelled, furtively, wraith, recuperate, admonish
3. a. gorgon b. centaur c. cyclops d. minotaur e. werewolf
4. weird, decision, courageous, accompany, were, approached, its, won't, crept, there, heels
5. a. whisky b. cotton c. Money d. weapons e. grain f. documents
6. a. actor b. designer c. builder d. doctor e. competitor f. crusader g. sensor h. gaoler i. finisher j. sailor k. eraser l. constrictor
7. a. appearance b. handkerchief c. skilful d. embarrassed e. propeller
8. a. between b. Between c. among d. Among e. between

Unit Nineteen:
1. a. smart and cunning b. coax, persuade c. rowdy young person d. boldness, daring e. suggest indirectly f. able to express oneself clearly g. escape by cleverness h. cautious
2. shrewd, audacity, wisdom, cajole, insinuate, trouble, articulate, elude, wary, hooligan
3. a. seize b. hesitant c. foolishness d. daring e. popular f. approve g. thoughtless
4. a. courageous b. ambitious c. generous d. famous e. conscious f. ambiguous g. advantageous h. anonymous i. serious j. various
5. a. cairn b. throng c. archipelago d. squadron e. index f. range g. truss h. canteen
6. a. outspoken b. stout c. elderly d. passed away e. intoxicated
7. a. revue b. confidant c. interstate d. internment e. moral

Unit Twenty:
1. a. hostile b. disagreement c. unbalanced d. boldness e. empty f. shocking g. strong h. fury
2. strapping, profoundly, belligerent, wrath, bleak, discord, grisly, audacity, tale, demented
3. a. head over heels b. lose your head c. heads will roll
4. a. muscular, sturdy b. ghastly, terrifying c. aggressive, hostile d. desolate, dreary e. insane, deranged
5. duke / duchess; baron / baroness; count / countess; emperor / empress; host / hostess; wizard / witch; priest / priestess; brother-in-law / sister-in-law; lad / lass; sir / madam; god / goddess
6. a. thieves b. king c. hatter d. judge e. miser f. queen g. Methuselah h. babe i. Job j. sentinel
7. a. whose b. its c. There's d. past e. too f. fewer g. practise h. among

CORRECTIONS

Top Skills Vocabulary
Therese Burgess